Resolving Conflict

Learning How You Both Can Win and Keep Your Relationship

Dale R. Olen, Ph.D.

A Life Skills Series Book

JODA Communications, Ltd.
Milwaukee, Wisconsin

Editor: Carolyn Kott Washburne
Design: Chris Roerden and Associates
Layout: Eileen Olen

ISBN 1-56583-012-1

Published by: JODA Communications, Ltd.
                10125 West North Avenue
                Milwaukee, WI 53226

PRINTED IN THE UNITED STATES OF AMERICA

"Pot Shots" reprinted by permission of
Ashleigh Brilliant, copyright © 1980.

Table of Contents

Introduction

to the
Life Skills Series

Nobody gets out alive! It isn't easy navigating your way through life. Your relationships, parents, marriage, children, job, school, church, all make big demands on you. Sometimes you feel rather ill-equipped to make this journey. You feel as if you have been tossed out in the cold without even a warm jacket. Life's journey demands considerable skill. Navigating the sometimes smooth, other times treacherous journey calls for a wide variety of tools and talents. When the ride feels like a sailboat pushed by a gentle breeze, slicing through the still waters, you go with the flow. You live naturally with the skills already developed.

But other times (and these other times can make you forget the smooth sailing), the sea turns. The boat shifts violently, driven by the waves' force. At those stormy moments, you look at your personal resources, and they just don't seem sufficient.

Gabriel Marcel, the French philosopher, wrote that the journey of life is like a spiral. The Greeks, he observed, viewed life as *cyclical*– sort of the same old thing over and over. The seasons came, went, and came again. History repeated itself. The Hebrews, on the other hand, saw life as *linear*–a pretty straight march toward a goal. You begin

5

at the Alpha point and end at Omega. It's as simple as that.

Marcel combined the two views by capturing the goal-oriented optimism of the Hebrews and the sobering reality of the Greeks' cycles. Life has its ups and downs, but it always moves forward.

To minimize the *downs* and to make the most of the *ups*, you need **Life Skills**. When you hike down the Grand Canyon, you use particular muscles in your back and legs. And when you trudge up the Canyon, you use other muscles. So too with life skills. You call on certain skills when your life spirals down, such as the skill of defeating depression and managing stress. When your life is on an upswing, you employ skills like thinking reasonably and meeting life head on.

This series of books is about the skills you need for getting through life. To get from beginning to end without falling flat on your face and to achieve some dignity and some self-satisfaction, you need **basic** life skills. These include:

1. Accepting yourself.
2. Thinking reasonably.
3. Meeting life head on.

With these three life skills mastered to some degree, you can get a handle on your life. Now, if you want to build from there, you are going to need a few more skills. These include:

4. Communicating.
5. Managing stress.
6. Being intimate.
7. Resolving conflict.
8. Reducing anger.
9. Overcoming fear.
10. Defeating depression.

If you have these ten skills up and running in your life, you are ready to face yourself, your relationships, your parents, your marriage, your children, your job and even God with the hope of handling whatever comes your way. Without these skills, you are going to bump into one stone wall after another. These skills don't take away the problems, the challenges and the hard times. But they do help you dig out of life's deep trenches and more fully *enjoy* the good times.

Life Skills can be learned. You have what it takes to master each of these skills–even if you feel you don't have the tiniest bit of the skill right now. But nobody can develop the skill for you. You have to take charge and develop it yourself. Your family, friends and community may be able to help you, but you are the center at which each skill has to start. Here is all you need to begin this learning process:

- Awareness.
- The desire to grow.
- Effort and practice.

Awareness begins the process of change. You have to notice yourself, watch your behavior and honestly face your strengths and weaknesses. You have to take stock of each skill and of the obstacles in you that might inhibit its growth.

Once you recognize the value of a skill and focus on it, you have to want to pursue it. The critical principle here, one you will see throughout this series, is *desire*. Your desire will force you to focus on the growing you want to do and keep you going when learning comes hard.

Finally, your *effort and practice* will make these **Life Skills** come alive for you. You can do it. The ten books in the **Life Skills Series** are tools to guide and encourage your progress. They are my way of being with you–cheering your efforts. But without your practice, what you find in these books will wash out to sea.

Working on these ten **Life Skills** won't get you through life without any scars. But the effort you put in will help you measure your life in more than years. Your life will be measured in the zest, faith, love, honesty and generosity you bring to yourself and your relationships.

I can hardly wait for you to get started!

Chapter One

The Skill of
Resolving Conflict

You may avoid serious illness in your life. You may remain free from car accidents and plane crashes. You may escape harm from floods, storms and plagues. But I guarantee you will not slip past the pain, stress and emotional trauma of *interpersonal conflict*. As long as your mind and emotions continue to function, you will find yourself embroiled in differences with other thoughtful and feeling people.

Conflict comes with the territory of living in a human world. To successfully maneuver your way from birth to death, you absolutely need the skill of resolving conflict. It really should stand with the other "3 Rs": reading, 'riting, 'rithmetic . . . and resolving conflict. You have manuals for the first three Rs. You study them in the classroom, you do homework, you take tests until you get it right. With conflict, your classroom is less formal – the home, the playground, the park, the store. Parents stand on the podium as your major professors. They teach without any manual. They demonstrate the skills for dealing – or not dealing – with conflict. This educational approach possesses much greater teaching power than any school classroom teacher could offer.

To balance what you learned early in life about interpersonal tensions, this book serves as your "conflict manual." In it I will show you how conflict works and what causes it in your life. By understanding the dynamics of conflict, you can more easily take charge of it and control it in your life. Knowledge leads to power. Understanding conflict will give you power over it. In this manual I will also offer you the necessary principles and tools to resolve conflict, so that you can develop more loving and peaceful relationships.

You've already learned some good habits and some bad habits regarding conflict. I want to reinforce the good ones and help you challenge and change the bad ones. I invite you to remain open to trying new ways of entering conflict and bringing it to a winning conclusion for you *and* the other person. By learning these principles and tools, you do a favor not only for yourself but also for all your friends, family, acquaintances and business associates.

Let's begin by looking at what causes conflict.

Chapter Two

Causes of Conflict

Conflict arises in many ways and spins off many intriguing dynamics. It adds spark and interest to life. It also causes great pain and hurt. It's the stuff of movies, novels and age-old stories. When all of the stories are narrated, and all the research on conflict is completed, one cause will stand out as the basis for all conflict. One element underlies every conflict experienced by every person who has or will ever live.

The basis of all conflict is *unmet needs*.

Today my wife and I had to buy a clothes washer and dryer. We had a need and entered a momentary relationship with a man who also had a need. Our need for these appliances matched his need to sell such appliances and earn a living. We got along just fine. Both our needs were met. The relationship lasted about 30 minutes without any conflict at all. The amount we paid fell within our expectations. The amount he received seemed to fall within his expectations.

Had he asked too much money for the washer and dryer, we

would have had a conflict. My need not to spend an "arm and a leg" on an unromantic household item would not have been met. I would have tried to negotiate him down to my range of spending. He would have resisted. Tense moments would have ensued. We may eventually have struck a deal where one of us would have felt like we won and the other lost. Had I felt the cost was still too high, I would have walked out of the store. Then we both would have lost.

In friendships and closer relationships the issue of *needs* sits right smack in the middle of things. If you meet each other's personal needs, you get along well. If you don't, you eventually get into a conflict over the unmet needs, or you simply end the relationship. If you have no needs, you have no conflicts. Of course, you will then be dead, I suspect.

Several reasons explain why your needs don't always get met. They involve

    1. How *aware* you are of your needs.

    2. Whether you *express* your needs or not.

    3. Whether the other person *responds* to your needs or not.

Depending on these three factors, you have a number of different emotional and behavioral responses that increase or decrease the amount of conflict in your life.

Let's look more closely at the three factors and their various combinations:

You're unaware of your needs, so you don't express them. The other can't respond to them. In this case, you don't even know you have a particular need. It lies outside the range of your conscious thoughts. Naturally, if you don't know your need, you can't express it and ask that it be met. The other person, of course, has no clue as to the need and so doesn't respond to it.

For example, Tom had a need for intimacy, but didn't know it. He sought sexual relationships with women. It looked like he was simply out to "make it" with whomever he could meet. But deep within him moved a need for psychological closeness. He was trying to meet that need by getting physically close to women, but finding such closeness not completely satisfying. As a result, Tom always felt a certain restlessness and dissatisfaction. He kept searching for something but didn't know what. Whatever he discovered did not seem enough. So he never stayed in a relationship very long. He was always in search. Entering and ending relationships as he did caused considerable conflict for Tom. His unrecognized need for intimacy was not being met.

You're aware of your need, but you don't express it. The other can't respond to it. June is aware of her need. She wants alone time with her husband – outside of the home. But she doesn't tell him that. She's afraid he won't want to do anything with her. And she believes it's selfish for her to have such a need. So she doesn't say anything. Yet she still expects him to respond to her unexpressed need. She thinks, "After all these years of marriage, he ought to know I need to get out of the house."

When he doesn't guess her need and fails to respond to it, she attempts to give him hints. She tries expressing the need *indirectly* through sighs or pouts or negative comments about "cabin fever." She feels hurt ("He doesn't notice what I need") when he doesn't pick up on her cues. Then she begins feeling resentful. This passive-aggressive reaction inevitably leads to tension and conflict in the relationship.

You're aware of your need, and you express it. But the other doesn't respond to it. This one hurts, because in a loving relationship you think the other will always respond with care to your every wish. You believe your request is reasonable and that the other wants to meet your need. So when he or she fails to do so, you feel some rejection.

The other may not respond to your need for two reasons: First, he may not have *recognized* or really heard your need, even though you thought you expressed it clearly. In this case you continue repeating your need, in ever stronger terms, trying to get him to notice. If he doesn't get it, you might use sarcasm, nagging and open resentment to get him to hear you. If all that fails, you withdraw in discouragement.

The second reason the other might not respond is he doesn't *want* to. Either he sees your needs conflicting with his own, or he sees your needs as too extravagant and unfulfillable. This also leads to hurt, discouragement, anger and withdrawal.

You're aware of your need, and you express it. The other responds to your need in parity. Here you keep score. "I'll do this for you, if you do that for me." Brothers and sisters engage in this strategy frequently. A sister asks her brother if he'd take the garbage out for her because she's late for her dance class. He says he'll do it if she makes a copy of her newest music tape for him.

While this can work for a while, it inevitably causes conflict, because one or both parties begin believing they are getting the "short end of the deal." The other person always seems to be ahead on the score card. When the other gets too far ahead of you, you become resentful and quit responding to his or her needs. More conflict ensues.

You're aware of your need, and you express it. The other responds to your need completely. In this instance you have peace and joy in your relationship. If you and your friend or loved one regularly express your needs and respond to each other's needs as best you can, your relationship proceeds smoothly. It continues as long as both of you feel your needs are being met. When your needs are no longer met by the other, you eventually end the relationship. Relationships do not continue unless *both* of you feel your needs are being met.

Relating in a win-lose manner causes conflict.

In our society we love the contest – "The thrill of victory, the agony of defeat." On the sports field, in the courtroom, in the corporate offices, on the school yard and in the classroom, winning and losing are as much a part of us as motherhood and apple pie. Naturally, then, we carry this attitude into our relationships.

From infancy on you have struggled in a win-lose, one-up/one-down world. Every time you work your way to one-up, you soon find yourself one-down. Then you work up again. When you bring this attitude to close personal relationships, you set the stage for conflict. If your needs are met and mine aren't, then you win and I lose. If I meet your need to sit and read, then I lose out on my need to go for a walk.

Thinking in terms of winning and losing doesn't work well in personal relationships. If you think in this way, you can be sure your relationships will be filled with conflict, unless, perhaps, you relate to someone who enjoys losing. Creating a win-lose relationship leads to *antagonistic* rather than *cooperative* relationships. In such a relationship both of you will keep score. You will alternate roles, with one being the "attacker" and the other the "defender." The battle results in a power struggle.

On the other hand, in a *cooperative* relationship you both feel like winners. You share your needs with each other and minister to those needs as best you can. You don't count the cost. You remain focused on pleasing and satisfying the other, knowing that the other is attempting to respond to your needs as well. You work for each other's happiness and feel good when the other achieves that delight.

The need for power in a relationship causes conflict.

Seeking to win or go one-up in a relationship can give you a sense of power. When you go one-down, you lose that feeling of power. You may be someone who needs to dominate a relationship, to feel in control of it, in order to feel good about yourself. If so, it helps to understand the effects of your need for power on your relationship.

Power usually comes from knowledge. It can come from brute force, but in most relationships it comes from knowledge. Whoever has the most information usually has the most power. Also, whoever has something the other wants or needs has the most power. For example, Al has more information about himself than Sheila has about him. Sheila has a need to be close to Al, which she can have if he would reveal more of himself. He chooses not to. He has power in this relationship because he has knowledge he's not sharing, and she seeks that knowledge.

Sheila knows her need and often asks Al what he's thinking or feeling. He always responds by saying, "Nothing much." His withdrawal – the mystery that surrounds him – keeps him protected and in power. He remains one-up because she never quite knows where she stands with him. She has to guess what he's thinking and feeling.

Al, however, falls into an interesting trap. He, too, wants intimacy. He wants both, intimacy and power. But he can't have both at the same time. For intimacy he and Sheila need a mutual partnership. They need to feel like equals. As long as he withholds information, they are not equals and cannot be intimate. If Al shares information, they can have intimacy, but he will then feel a loss of power and feel quite vulnerable. If he finds vulnerability too uncomfortable, he won't share, thus maintaining a power, one-up/one-down relationship. Conflict results because neither Al nor Sheila will feel intimate, something they both need.

Conflict happens when you and another both try to *persuade* each other of the correctness of your position.

Here's that win-lose situation again. You and your friend are both trying hard to win. You are both convinced you're right, and your goal is to convince the other. Beating the other into intellectual submission seems all important at the moment. You certainly don't listen to each other, because each of you is preparing your wisdoms while the other rambles on. There will be no persuading you of another position. You know you're right!

These arguments accelerate in volume and emotion. Why? Because both of you are becoming increasingly frustrated. Your wonderfully lucid arguments don't seem to be convincing the other. She isn't telling you how right you are. She's just as stubborn as she always is. Nothing has changed. So you up the ante. You yell and scream, demanding that she see your point of view and agree. Ashleigh Brilliant ©, author of *I Have Abandoned My Search for Truth, and Am Now Looking for A Good Fantasy* (Woodbridge Press, 1980), once wrote: "It always helps prove how right you are if you wave your arms and jump and scream." You both believe this and end up in a major yelling match. Was anybody persuaded?

Conflict occurs when you disagree and/or try solving the other's problem *before* you understand the person.

You get mired in conflict when the normal order of communication breaks down. Communication that works follows this pattern:

1. You hear what the other is saying.
2. You understand the other thoroughly.
3. You appreciate and feel the other's position.
4. You can then agree or disagree with one another.
5. You can problem solve your differences or offer suggestions for the other's problems.

Conflict breaks out when step 4 or 5 comes before 1, 2 and 3. I can't tell you how many arguments I have stopped in my office because people didn't *understand* each other before disagreeing or problem solving. First of all, other people don't often want you to agree or disagree. They just want you to get the message. Second, more often they don't want you to give them advice about what to do. If you listen to people asking to talk, they rarely ask you to tell them what to do. They say, "Can I talk with you for a minute?" Even when they come into my office for counseling, they rarely say, "I hope you can tell me what to do." If you attempt to solve other people's problems when all they want is for you to listen, conflict results because their need for understanding is not being met.

Specific mental activities you go through cause conflict with others.

So far, we have looked at the basic, global causes of conflict. In every conflict you will recognize the issue of unmet needs, the sense of winning and losing, the need to persuade and the inability to understand the other. You also generate conflict because of responses inside of you, mostly in the way you think. See if you use any of the mental activities described below. If you do, then be willing to declare them your enemy and drive them from your mind. They never help you deal well with conflict.

1. Polarizing

This happens when you need to persuade and convince someone who doesn't agree with you. Imagine you and I are both interior designers. We disagree on the color of a wall. I say it's beige, and you say it's tan. Oh, my gosh, you didn't agree with me. Now I must convince you of just how beige that wall actually is. "It really is beige," I say. "In fact, if you look closely, you can see a hint of white in it that gives it that beige look."

You're not buying that for a second. You counter, "Look, that wall is so tan, if it has a hint of anything in it, it shows traces of brown." You see, each of us is beginning to move further from the other's position. We begin to overstate our own position in order to convince the other. Of course, our little overstatements don't seem to work, so we inflate and distort them even more.

I say, "You know, that wall really is off-white toward the beige side." You reply, "Actually, the wall is brown with a hint of tan." I plow forward, disregarding accuracy and reality for the sake of winning the argument: "Darn it, the wall is pure white. It's the whitest wall I've ever seen." You're just as adamant: "This wall is dark brown. In fact, on closer inspection, you could call it black. Yes, it's black, black as coal."

This is called "polarization." We have a minor difference. But because we each want to convince the other of how right we are, we have to move *away* from each other's view and intensify our own.

2. Dramatizing

In order to convince you of how right I am about the wall, I add drama, color and exaggeration. You do the same. Beige becomes white, and tan becomes black. We actually distort our own view of reality. Here's the kicker when we dramatize: We begin to believe our own distortions. Pretty soon we are arguing about something neither one of us believes to be true.

You see this frequently with kids. You catch a child lying and call her on it. She objects. As you press the issue, she makes up more lies. As the debate over lying goes on, she becomes incensed that you don't trust her. In pleading her innocence and honesty, she comes to believe she always tells the truth. How dare you for not believing her. Before the argument is over, she's angry at you for not trusting her. She's convinced she didn't lie and that you're simply an out-of-touch parent. The distortion becomes the reality.

In many arguments I have seen, both parties are basically fighting over their "hallucinations." Reality has little to do with the conflict.

3. Personalizing

After you have polarized your conflict, you have no place to go except to begin attacking the other person. In our interior design debate, where can we go after I have the wall white and you have it black? We can go after each other. So I say to you, "There's no point in talking with you. You're so stubborn anyway." You come back with, "Oh yeah. Well, you're so color-blind, I don't know how you even got into this business." At which point, I go for the jugular: "You know, you're just like your mother . . . . "

Now we have lost sight of the original difference. We're going after each other. The issue is no longer the color or a wall, but which ego can get in the last word, the last cut, humbling the opponent into silence. When the conflict reaches this level, you're in serious trouble. A line gets crossed when you leave the arena of substantive differences for personal attacks. Often you cannot return from that position. You can forgive me for my poor judgment regarding the beige (or was it the tan?) wall. But you might find it harder to let go of the remark I made about your mother.

If you find yourself personalizing a difference, realize that you are probably acting out of frustration. You can't get your point across through reason and statements of "reality," so you have to hit the other over the head with a verbal hammer to get her attention. Unfortunately when you do that, she focuses more on the pain at the top of her head than on your important message to her.

4. Perceiving the other as a "bad guy"

Interpersonal conflict often involves *misperceptions*. Because you don't understand what your friend means, you begin to interpret his messages. In a conflicted situation your interpretations will lean toward the negative side. This person is opposing you, therefore he must be your enemy. You don't know why he's acting against you. So you guess. It must be he doesn't like you, or he's out to get your job. The more you view him with a sinister eye, the more villainous he becomes.

As a witness to thousands of interpersonal conflicts over the years, I have yet to meet the real "bad guys." I have seen many people *perceived* as bad by the other combatant. But the more you understand how people think and respond to stress and difficulty, the more you realize they are not "bad" but in need. They have histories that lead them to respond the way they do. They have unmet needs but know of no other way to get those needs taken care of than by arguing with you.

When you flip the misperception issue over, you will realize what I'm saying. The other person in the conflict perceives you as the "bad guy," just as you perceive him as the bad guy. He actually thinks you have evil motives, that you don't like him, that you're selfish or conceited. At the time of the conflict, he doesn't like you much, either. He thinks you're out to hurt him. Now you know that's not true. You see yourself as a decent person, who has a civil – even a caring – heart. You are not a sinister individual, out for the kill.

These misperceptions of one another as the enemy alienate a relationship quickly. You both perceive each other as out to hurt rather than care. In order to protect yourself from possible hurt, you either withdraw or strike first. Both strategies harm the relationship and increase the level of conflict.

5. Turning desires and needs into demands

Let's say you have a need for companionship. You seek someone to do things with – go to the movies, to a ball game, out for a meal and so on. Just having the need won't cause any conflict. The conflict arises when you expect or demand that a specific person fill your need. If you don't expect your mother to be your constant companion when you go out, you won't get into a fight with her when she declines your invitation to go shopping. You won't get conflicted with work associates or casual neighbors, if you don't demand that they fill your needs. But you will get upset and angry with your wife, if you demand that she be your companion and she doesn't comply.

Early in relationships, you give one another freedom. You make no demands. You have only hope, desires or wishes. If the other fails to respond, you don't apply much meaning to it. You simply accept the difference. But as your relationship progresses, gets more serious and more committed, you begin to rely on each other for the fulfillment of your personal needs. Your wishes gradually turn to demands. You begin expecting your spouse to be there for you, to make you his or her top priority, to take time with you, to remember all the special occasions, to be sensitive and caring, warm and loving. When you expect or demand your needs be filled by a specific person, and they don't get filled, you become angry.

In these instances your anger arises out of your hurt. You feel badly that the other has failed to recognize or meet your need. You then turn your attention to him, and become angry because "he should have wanted to go out with me tonight." Your anger also serves as a more dramatic form of communicating with him. Maybe he just didn't recognize your need. You think, "If I say it louder and with more force, maybe he'll get it." Of course, your anger pushes him further away from you and makes it more difficult for him to listen to your need and to respond to it.

As you know from your own experience, this conflict business can get very messy. It feels like a maze filled with cobwebs and dead ends. Once it starts, it seems as though it has a life of its own, carrying you to more and more complex traps. Once you're in, it's often tough to get out.

Fortunately, there are ways to move through the conflicts of your life and reach significant states of peace and harmony with those you love. To achieve tranquility, though, you need to give up many of your instinctive responses to conflict, especially those that have not worked for you.

In the following chapter I will describe for you the principles and tools you need to resolve the conflicts that occur in your daily life. With these tools conflict will become an opportunity for growth and harmony rather than hurt and discord.

Chapter Three

Principles and Tools for Resolving Conflict

I wish I could give you a simple formula for resolving all the conflicts that arise in your life. You just plug this formula in, follow the steps – one, two, three – and the conflict is resolved. I will give you such a formula, but I can't guarantee it will always work, simply because I can't guarantee how the other person will respond. I also cannot be sure that in the heat of the moment you will follow the formula. I know *I* have trouble following it in the midst of a conflict. I'm much better at knowing what I "should have done" after the fact.

So I'll give you the formula anyway and hope you can apply it successfully in most situations. First, I'll tell you what it is in its most simple and general form. Then we'll go through it piece by piece.

To resolve the interpersonal conflicts in your life:

- You need to communicate well, paying close attention to the needs of one another.
- You need to bring to your conflicts a set of specific attitudes and beliefs that are not defensive and not aggressive.
- You need to take definite action in response to conflict.

Now let's look at each of these three steps in detail.

Communicate well.

Principle 1

In the midst of conflict slow down so you can learn rather than persuade.

Listening and understanding does not mean the other person wins and you lose. You don't need to shout louder, talk faster or verbally beat the other into submission and silence to win an argument. Listening quietly does not mean you have nothing to say because the other is right and you have lost the verbal match. Slowing down to listen helps relieve the other person of her need to send you a message. Once she feels you have understood her, she is more able and more likely to understand you.

Judy gets angry with you because you failed to tell her about the deadline for the job. She starts hitting you over the head with her words. You immediately fight back. The conflict escalates. If you don't defend yourself, you're afraid Judy will think she was right and you were wrong.

We have no word in the English language to describe what Judy is doing when she expresses herself in anger. The best way to describe her behavior is to call it "over-standing." She is standing over you, metaphorically speaking, making herself bigger than life so that you notice and pay attention. If you don't pay attention, she makes herself even bigger. That's what anger does. It inflates her, so you notice and hear what she has to say. In fact, when she "over-stands" you, the best way – the only way – to respond is through *understanding*. If she over-stands you and you over-stand her, you both end up shouting and frustrated because she never got your point nor you hers.

Look what understanding does for this potentially explosive situation. By receiving her angry message, she knows you got it. She is then able to let go of her need to tell you how you goofed up. At that point she can become more receptive to your explanation of why you didn't mention the job deadline to her. Because you understand her, she is better able to understand you.

Principle 2

Create a *Giver-Receiver* rhythm of communication when you have differences.

Understanding Judy before you try persuading her helps create this Giver-Receiver rhythm of communication. Most conflicts establish a non-rhythm of Giver-Giver. You and Judy are both attempting to give messages at the same time, with neither person doing much listening or receiving. You can't play catch if both of you are trying to throw fast balls to each other at the same time. You can't communicate if you're both verbally winding-up and delivering, aiming for the other's head.

It's up to you to create the Giver-Receiver rhythm at the moment of conflict. You can't depend on Judy doing it. She's intent on giving, or sending you her important message. Even though you think your message is equally important (or probably even more important than hers), you need to bite your tongue, take a deep breath and listen. Throughout the conflict pay attention to what Judy does. When she wants to be the Giver, then you become the Receiver. When you think she has completed her giving and is capable of receiving, then you can become the giver. You need a great deal of flexibility to manage this rhythm. You also need patience, because you will want to jump in and convince Judy of your position. Realize that neither of you will be very convincing if you are not listening to one another.

So slow down your need to send messages and listen first. Make sure you understand, and let Judy know you understand. Then you can present your "truth" to her, hoping she will understand. For more on the skill of effective communication, read the **Life Skills Series** book *Communicating*.

Principle 3

Don't get hooked by people's first statements to you. Keep searching for the real and deeper meaning of what they say.

The first statements in a conflict serve the purpose of shock. They attempt to get your attention. Usually those statements are inaccurate, exaggerated and distorted. Unfortunately, those statements not only get your attention, they hook you emotionally. You take them seriously. You hold onto those words and find it difficult to hear anything after that first shot.

"If that's the way you feel, then you take care of the kids yourself. I'm out of here," shouts John. "Oh, he's threatening divorce," thinks Sue. In the post-argument debate, Sue continually brings up John's threat of divorce. "You're talking about divorce over such a dinky incident. I can't believe you have so little commitment to our marriage." He tries to explain, "Look I didn't mean I wanted a divorce. It's just that I have had it with your criticism of the way I parent. I can never do anything right when it comes to the kids, according to you."

"But you said, 'I'm out of here,'" Sue presses on. "That sounds like divorce to me." Sue is hooked on John's opening statement. She won't let go of it. Her belief is that once the words have been spoken, they must mean literally what they sound like. No. In his upset and his desire to get away from her criticism, John expressed his frustration and his dislike of criticism in a quick, impulsive and somewhat dramatic way. She took his words as a perfect expression of what he wanted to say.

This was Sue's mistake. In the heat of the argument, she grabbed onto a literal interpretation of John's comments. She needed to patiently wade through all his words in order to get to the core message of what he was trying to communicate. John was not that in touch with his deepest feelings, thoughts and needs. So his first effort at expressing those deeper realities wasn't very accurate. In other words, at the moment, John didn't know himself well enough to match his words perfectly with his deepest feelings. It often takes time and a number of tries to say what you mean. It may have taken him three or four attempts to actually state what he really meant.

When you are in conflict, then, do not latch onto the first expression a person makes as his or her most accurate. Just because she said certain words doesn't mean she really meant them. "But," you say, "she must have meant them. They just popped out. She must have been thinking this way for a long time." No. She is making the effort to communicate what is deepest in her, but she isn't completely in touch with herself. So she has to say it a number of times until she gets her words to accurately reflect her heart. That's extremely difficult to do when she and you are emotionally wrapped up in a conflict.

So be patient with her. Don't hold onto her first, second or even third attempts to articulate what she deeply feels. Just accept them as attempts to communicate. Stay with her in an understanding mode until she can say what she really means. This attitude keeps you in a listening, non-judging framework that greatly helps you resolve the conflict with your friend or partner.

Bring specific attitudes to conflict.

Principle 4

Move into rather than away from conflict.

Although the majority of people deal with conflict by withdrawal or submission, I want to encourage you to face it and work it through right away. Your history with conflict may tell you it's dangerous and should be avoided. You may remember that as a child conflict seemed traumatic and violent. People got hurt emotionally and, perhaps, physically. No way do you want to get into those hurting and exhausting situations now. So you avoid conflict, believing the same will happen today that happened when you were a child.

Please, dispute the belief you might have that says: "If it happened this way when I was a child, it will happen the same way now." If you use the skills of resolving conflict, the same thing won't happen today that happened years ago. Back then, you didn't possess the skills to resolve conflict effectively. Maybe your parents, brothers, sisters and relatives didn't have those skills, either. No wonder, then, that entering conflict seemed to make matters worse rather than better. But now you can bring new skills to your conflicts. You can slow yourself down and listen patiently much better than before. You can communicate and respond to your partner's needs. You know better ways to think, healthier attitudes to bring to the conflict and more productive actions to take to resolve the conflict so both of you feel like winners.

Armed with your new skills, entering conflict can lift your relationship to higher levels of intimacy rather than causing an ever-deepening rift between you. You can approach the other with confidence, believing you have it within you to bring peace to this relationship. The pain of past conflict need not be repeated in your present circumstances. By approaching the other with the skills described in this book, you can experience the satisfaction and relief of facing your differences, understanding and respecting each other's positions and attempting to respond positively to each others' needs.

Principle 5

Realize that objective truth will never be known.

Certainly you want to be right. You have a good grasp on reality. Your senses don't deceive you. It's beyond your imagination how Jim could see the situation any differently. So you fight him over the facts, over what actually happened. Many times arguments over the facts occur when you're debriefing some other argument. This becomes the argument within the argument.

You can be arguing over any issue out there – the kids, money, relatives, work assignments. The argument ends. Later, you get together and begin discussing your argument. You start disagreeing on who started it, what you actually said and how you both acted during the argument. Each of you has a point of view that makes it sound like two completely different arguments. You cannot agree on the facts of what actually happened.

At that point realize objective truth will never be known. You both saw and heard different things. Ask yourself if it makes any difference, really, if you said "Boo" first or he said "Baa" first. It's almost never worth having a second argument over some fact just to solve a first argument. Learn to "let it go." Your need to be right will almost always interfere with the resolution of the conflict.

Principle 6

Realize the other actually believes he or she is right.

Although you "know" that objectivity, truth, justice and fairness are all on your side, it helps to realize the other person believes the same. It's hard to imagine, but he actually thinks he treated you fairly. He really believes he has been more attentive to you lately, that he has spent more time with you, that he hasn't been out with the guys as much. He believes you have treated him poorly, that you are always critical of him, that you have gotten more touchy and that you don't understand him as well as you used to.

Years ago I had a dispute with a group of business associates. I felt they totally misjudged my position and falsely accused me of making decisions independently of them. I was outraged. In my view I had gone over and above the call of duty to include them. How could they possibly think such things of me? We parted ways. I couldn't believe their perception of me. For a long time afterward I felt angry with these men because they were so far off the mark. But gradually I came to realize that they honestly believed their point of view. They thought they were completely "in the right." Because they did, they responded accordingly. They actually thought I was cutting into their territory in some way and they felt a need to protect themselves. No wonder they acted as they did. They fully believed their "misperceptions" of me.

By understanding their view that they were right and I was wrong, I found myself more able to accept their behavior toward me. To this day I still don't like the way they responded, and I wish they knew my "truth," but at least I don't interpret them as evil and awful men. They simply believed something to be true and acted on it. They may have been men limited in their perception of reality, but they weren't bad people. In fact, they were good people, who, I believe, just didn't have a full picture of reality – according to me!

Principle 7

Free yourself from *blaming* the other. Realize it takes two of you to make a conflict happen.

When you try to re-create the cause of a conflict, inevitably the other person "started it." Of course, you are partially to blame. But you wouldn't have started yelling if she didn't first give you that critical look. Blaming the other is a way of deflecting the conflict and laying it at the other's feet.

Ninety percent of the couples I have seen in counseling over the years start their first session with me by blaming each other for the problem. They want me to "fix" the other person. "If he could get over his depression and anger, then we'd have a good marriage," she complains. "If you could figure out why she is so cold and unaffectionate, and she could warm up, things would be 100 percent improved," he argues. You see, if it's the other's fault, then the blamer doesn't need to do any work. The therapist will fix "the deficient one," and all will be fine.

To change a relationship that's in conflict, you need to believe that *both* of you caused the problem. You are not clean. You are a major part of the conflict. In fact, the other person believes you are the biggest part of the problem. You need not accept *all* the responsibility for what's gone wrong. That would be as unrealistic as placing all the blame on the other. You simply need to acknowledge that both of you created the monster that now separates you.

Once you realize and accept your part in the problem, you will become more motivated to change the way you react to the other. For instance, if part of your response is to back away when she gets critical, then you may decide to engage her at those moments and try simply understanding her without taking her comments too personally. You might try instead to figure out what her needs are.

Let's say an occasion arises where your partner, Alice, is being critical. You realize you're part of the problem. Perhaps you don't listen as well as you might. So you make a change, attempting to listen better and not take her comments too personally. But she continues to criticize you. Her continued criticism, despite your change, now proves to you more fully than before that the problem really is hers. You have attempted to change but she has remained the same. So, you think, it's her turn to change now.

You're doing your part, you think, and she's not doing hers. So why should you continue doing yours? Because that's what allows her to change gradually. Keep on doing your part. Don't quit just because she continues being critical. Stay with it. If you change, eventually she will too. The two of you are like a machine with several gears, all of which work together. When you change the speed of one gear, all the gears are forced to change speeds as well. In human conflict the same thing happens. When you change, she is forced to make a change, too. It may not happen right away, but a change will take place. Don't quit your change, though, because you are not seeing results yet. Stay with it until she sees your change or believes it. Then she will respond.

Principle 8

**Bring a light heart and a flexible mind
to all your conflicts.**

Rigid and serious thinkers have much more trouble with conflict than their opposites. I know it's not easy to change your thinking from "demanding and grave" to "adaptable and light-hearted." But try.

Most conflicts you get into are not that important. They may seem so at the moment, but in the wider view of things, they usually shrink in size.

With children, in particular, you need a light heart and a ton of patience. When you take your differences with your children too seriously, you damage the relationships. The kids pull away from you. Is it worth it? See the humor in the crazy things they do and say. Being too serious with kids strikes a death blow to your relationship with them and can give you ulcers as well!

One way of maintaining a flexible mind is by keeping your priorities straight. Your relationship stands as the number one priority. With your serious and rigid mind, you chip away at the relationship by insisting on what is right and just. When the world doesn't comply with your demands about how things should be, you become angry. And your anger drives away your friend or partner.

Now I'm not saying you must learn to give in on every issue. Submission doesn't help relationships, either. But by loosening up you will be able to discuss differences rather than argue them. Discussing brings you together; arguing will drives you apart.

So lighten up. Kick back a little bit. Value what's important, namely your relationship with your partner, your kids, your boss, employees and friends. The issues can be discussed. But accept, graciously, that everyone believes he or she is right. And anyway, the truth may never be fully known.

Principle 9

During a conflict, know that the other person's words make a statement about him or her, not about you.

This non-defensive attitude will help you greatly when you face conflict. It gives you some distance between yourself and the one acting aggressively toward you. In conflict the two of you get into each other's space. Your boundaries are not clear and clean. So you need psychological distance. You've often heard the advice, "Don't take it personally." That's what I mean here. What the other person says is a statement about him or her, not a statement about you.

You want to keep yourself distinct from what the other is saying, even if it is about you. I know it's hard not to take it personally if Janet says to you, "You're a real jerk, you know." That seems like a statement about you, right? At that moment I want you to translate the message differently. Try to realize that when Janet makes that statement, she is really trying hard to get through to you. She is upset with you about something. You probably know what. She is inflating herself so that you notice her and pay attention to this important thing she has to tell you. She is using a sledge hammer to get your attention.

As I said earlier, don't take her first statements too literally or seriously. She's struggling to say what is really bothering *her*. If she's upset, then *she* is the one with a problem. The issue is hers, not yours. Your job is simply to receive and understand *her* problem. After you understand it, you can decide if you have a problem, too.

One caution about taking this attitude: Never say to another person, "That's *your* problem, not *mine*." You will always trigger a more angry response by making that comment. Such a statement tells the other person that you don't care. You're not going to entertain what she's saying to you. You're not even going to carry on any discussion about it. That remark shuts the other person out. It drives her crazy. She will become more angry, and the conflict will accelerate.

Realize that what Janet says to you is simply her effort to communicate with you in a powerful and dramatic way. You certainly don't appreciate her calling you names, but she's trying hard, and with some clumsiness, to get your attention and express whatever pain she feels. Approaching her "attacks" this way helps you be less defensive and attacking in return. Simply receive her. And then watch her tone down her language and gradually become more and more reasonable. Often you will find that the other person actually apologizes for coming on so strongly, especially if you have listened well and understood the need, the pain and upset she felt.

Principle 10

Realize that another's words do not make or change *your* reality.

This belief goes along with the one we just talked about. You cannot give the other person's words too much power in your life. When Janet called you a jerk, her words were not creative. Because she said it, you didn't, therefore, become a jerk. You either were a jerk or not, independently of her calling you one.

There's a theological belief here that might help you psychologically. The very first message the Bible presents is that God's word is creative. Whenever God spoke, according to the Bible, creation happened. "God said, 'Let there be light,' and there was light. God said, 'Let there be creatures of the sea' and so they were." Whenever God spoke, something was created. The same is not true for you and me. Just because Janet speaks, she does not create your reality, unless you let her words have that kind of power.

Again, her words make a statement about her, not you. Calling you a jerk doesn't make you a jerk, and it doesn't make her a jerk, either. You don't want to get into calling her back what she called you. Remember the kids' retort to name-calling? "I'm rubber, you're glue. Whatever you say bounces off of me and sticks to you." That's not what I'm talking about here. Janet's words tell you she is upset and wants you to hear her. That's the statement she is making about herself. Calling you a jerk gets your attention and doesn't make either of you a jerk.

Now when she tells you, for example, that you're egocentric and selfish, again that doesn't make you so. But it is helpful for you to hear her point of view and then compare it to your own experience. Perhaps her view matches your reality, even partially. If it does, then you can thank her for helping you see something about yourself. If it doesn't match anything in you, then she is simply mistaken and you can let her message go as a perception of hers that doesn't fit your perception.

These two attitudes – whatever someone says about you is a statement about him or her in some way; and another person's words do not create your reality – will help you listen to the other in a non-defensive way. These beliefs give you some space so you can listen without feeling threatened. The other is simply expressing something about him or herself. Fine. You can listen, receive the message and let the other know you got it. Your understanding relieves the other of anger and upset. It generates an atmosphere of calm, which leads to productive conversation, the resolution of differences and the satisfaction of needs.

Take Action.

Principle 11

**Stay with the present issue;
do not use the past as ammunition.**

This takes some discipline. But it keeps the waters clear and clean. Often when you want to make a point more dramatically, you call in past faults and problems. You say things like, "And furthermore, back in 1978 you said . . . ," or "You do this all the time. I can name at least five other times you did . . . ," and then you proceed to name them.

So stick with the present issue. Don't tell stories from the past. If you do, you hurt your own case, because you get tied up in arguing the facts and interpretations of an event ten years old. This principle should be obvious, but it's one of the most frequently violated in the heat of conflict. Resolve not to allow the past to interfere with present conflicts.

I don't want to suggest that you can never talk about the past. At certain times two people may need to deal with the past. But if you're in a here-and-now conflict, then stay with it. Don't bring in the past while a present conflict is in progress. Deal with past hurts and differences separately. When you discuss the past, you need to slow down your conversation. First try to fully receive the other's view. Then share your own. Apologies and expressions of forgiveness are often necessary to resolve past differences. But the best way to resolve the past is to not let the same behaviors continue in the present. Most of the time people hold onto the past because the present is no different. So you may talk about the past to alter the present. Just don't use the past as ammunition in your present debates.

Principle 12

Never attack the other person. Keep away from his or her vulnerable spots.

As I explained earlier, when you get into a conflict, you try to persuade the other of your position by using drama. When you cannot dramatize any further, you begin to attack the person. Don't do that. Inevitably you weaken the relationship.

In more intimate relationships you learn each other's vulnerabilities. Ted knew that the way to get to his wife, Gloria, was by making statements about her weight. In the midst of a conflict he would inevitably say how undisciplined she was about food. Gloria knew that Ted prided himself on his career climb to the top. In fights she would remind him of how far he still had to go and how many of his colleagues had already passed him by.

Such attacks push each party further away from the other. Over time you learned how sensitive the other person is in certain areas precisely because you committed yourselves to a close relationship. You learned about each other by being intimate. You cannot turn around now and use that intimacy against the other. When you share your sensitivities and limitations, you trust your weaknesses are safe with him or her. You cannot violate that trust by using such sacred information against the other in a time of conflict.

Remember, you want to maintain the priority of the relationship over "winning" the argument. You can do so by recognizing that you care about the other person even though you disagree with him. Years ago I heard the phrase "carefronting." When differences appear, you want to "carefront" the other rather than "confront." Confrontation puts you on opposite sides. If he argues with you and you believe he doesn't care, you get more defensive and attacking in return. But if he differs with you and you know he cares, then you don't mind. Your relationship is not threatened.

Try this if you find your confrontations turning to personal attacks. Start by letting each other know you care about the other. No matter what you talk about, it will not affect that basic care and love that exists between you. Then have your discussion of differences. Conflicts about ideas or behaviors don't cause difficulty as long as you don't feel you are personally being threatened or your relationship is being threatened. If you can assure each other of your love and care, then you can reasonably discuss your differences.

It's not possible to hit another person while you're hugging him or her. I'm not saying you should literally be hugging the other while discussing differences. But you get the idea. One couple told me they found their discussions went much more gracefully when they decided to sit *next* to each other rather than *across* from each other. Most conflicts need not threaten the basic relationship. You need to reaffirm the strength of your love and caring; then you can differ on all the little things. If basic respect and love are not there, then your differences will turn into personal attacks that irreparably damage the relationship.

Principle 13

When presenting a difficulty to your partner, own your own problem and talk about *you,* not the other.

Who's got the problem when your husband spends big money on antiques while you're trying desperately to save some dollars? Whose problem is it when your son keeps switching the channels with the remote control and you're getting annoyed with him? Who's got the problem when a work colleague dominates the meeting by talking incessantly and you grow impatient? In all these instances *you* have the problem, not the other person. Your husband has no problem spending all that money. Your son enjoys flipping channels every ten seconds. And your co-worker loves to hear himself chatter on. *You* have problems with these people doing things you don't like. These are your problems, not theirs.

When addressing these people, present the problem as yours, not theirs. Talk about the problem *you* are having with their behavior. Remember, they don't see themselves as having a problem. If you weren't upset about what they did, they would think everything was just fine. If something done by another person bothers you, then the problem is always yours. Certainly the other person may have his or her own set of problems, but the basic issue of conflict here is that *you* are bothered by whatever it is the other person is doing or not doing.

You have two ways of dealing with your husband's spending. You can make the problem his by saying: "What's the matter with *you* anyway? Don't *you* realize we don't have that kind of money to be spending foolishly on antiques? When are *you* going to grow up?" This is called sending a "you message." You aim your statements at your husband, attacking him and his behavior.

The second way you can respond is by sending him an "I message." Here you concentrate on *your* problem with his behavior. You say, "I become so worried over money. I see we have so many bills and the kids' college education is only a few years away. When you buy all those antiques, I become even more nervous. I really want to start saving some money every month. Can you understand my feelings, and would you work with me to help me save?" It takes a little longer to say all that. You need to use a few more words, but you now have a chance of being heard.

When you send "you messages," your husband will rarely hear you. He will experience your words as an attack. He will immediately become defensive and probably attack back. With both of you attacking, the explosive argument is inevitable. But if you talk about yourself and the problem you are having with his spending, he may be able to hear you. You're not accusing him of being an awful person; you're just telling him how worried you get about money matters.

Learn to talk about yourself when you "have a problem" with someone else. When you're bothered by someone else's behavior, then the problem is yours. Present it that way. Start by telling how you feel and what happens to you when your son flips the channels or your co-worker talks too much. In this way you invite the other person to actually help you resolve your problem. In fact, you're sharing your need with the other and asking that he or she minister to your need. By sharing in this way, you make your "confrontations" much more gentle and easier for the other to receive and respond to without feeling put down or accused.

Principle 14

In a conflict, keep your statements reality-based.
Do not dramatize in order to make a point.

By now this principle should be evident. I repeat it here just to complete the picture of how you want to present yourself in a conflict. Stay with reality. When you dramatize, you distort the real picture, and eventually you start believing your exaggeration.

You can dramatize by over- or under-stating the facts of a case. "I've told you a million times . . . . " "You *never* call to say 'hi.'" "It drives me *crazy* when you do that." Rather, simply keep on presenting the real picture. Give "just the facts, ma'am."

You can also dramatize by making threats you don't intend to carry out: "I've had it in this marriage. I'm seeing my lawyer tomorrow." "You're grounded for the next year." "I don't know why I'm working for a boss like you." These powerful expressions don't usually get forgotten by those who hear them. They continue to be recalled for years.

Another form of drama to avoid is name-calling. You do this out of frustration. You can't make your point, so you try to win by knocking down the other person. You can do this directly by saying, " You dummy. You stupid idiot. You lazy fool." Or you can do it indirectly by making comments like, "What the heck is the matter with you, anyway?" (implying something is clearly the matter with you); "You ought to go talk to a shrink!" (meaning, "You're crazy"); "You never make any sense at all." (translated as "You're dumb").

As best you can, then, stick with the facts. Don't exaggerate them. Stay with your problem. Don't attack the other person. And don't call the other names, directly or indirectly.

Principle 15

Deal with issues *immediately.*

When you don't resolve conflicts right away, they get put in the pressure cooker of your mind. You think about them. You mull them over. You make up monologues of what you'd really like to tell John.

But you never do it. Eventually another conflict pops up. You don't deal with that one either. You hold it in. Now you have two problems with John. Then three and four. Finally some dinky little thing happens. John forgets to turn out a light, and you blow up. All this time you have been pulling away from John, putting more and more distance between the two of you.

Getting into the issues as they come up keeps them small. And that's what you want – small issues that can be resolved in a few minutes. Discussing things immediately keeps them in perspective and manageable. John tells Beth, as he walks out the door in the morning, that he's playing tennis after work for an hour and invited the other three guys over for a beer and a sandwich. He will be home around 6:30. Goodbye.

Beth gets upset with John. He should have told her earlier, she thinks. She doesn't know if he expects her to make the sandwiches. She doesn't like it when he simply announces his plans rather than consulting with her. But she doesn't say anything. All day she mulls it over, stewing about John's insensitivity. She talks to her friend about it, getting more angry as she discusses her "chauvinistic husband."

When he comes home that evening without the guys (they decided to go to their own homes), she hits the ceiling. A major fight breaks out. Had she dealt with the issue right away in the morning, it would have been resolved before it got to "international crisis" status. Had she responded immediately, she would have stopped John as soon as he announced his plans. She would have told him right away how she was feeling and what she needed. If he had gotten out of the door before she could get in touch with her own reactions, then she would have called him at work and discussed it right away. By doing so, she would have been free from the issue the rest of the day and could have gotten on with her own work.

Although the general principle is to deal with issues immediately, there is one exception. If you tend to react with anger very quickly and impulsively, then you might want to slow down your response and put a little time between a conflict and your verbal response. You might need to walk away from a conflict for 15 minutes and then come back to deal with it. You can always tell the other, "Look, I really have a problem with what you just did. I need about 15 minutes to cool down a bit, and then I'd like to talk with you about this." Take the 15 minutes and then do it.

Usually people with impulsive anger need a little time and space to cool down before they begin talking about issues. By giving them that space, you have a much better chance of resolving the issue quickly and reasonably.

Principle 16

Deal with issues directly, not indirectly.

Remember, conflicts arise because your needs or the other's are not being met. You deal directly with conflicts, then, by telling the other what you need. But you have to tell. You cannot make the other person *guess*. Indirect problem-solving almost never works. In this approach you are saying to the other, "Look, I'm not going to tell you what I need. Instead, you have to guess. If you guess right, I'll reward you by acting nicely toward you. But if you guess wrong, I will punish you by pouting, by creating tension in the relationship and in general by making your contact with me miserable."

Don't get into that game. If you have a need, tell it to your partner. Ask for help with *your* problem. But don't try communicating your need passively through subtle behaviors, forcing the other to decipher your communication.

On the other side of this issue you may see your partner communicating her needs in an indirect way. Try to get her to communicate more directly. Invite her to share with you what she needs. The common way of doing this is to ask, "Jean, is anything wrong?" Jean will often respond with a simple "No." But you know something is wrong. So you ask again. She denies again, but goes on pouting and being distant.

I would suggest you not ask, "Is anything wrong?" when the other tends to communicate indirectly. It makes it too easy for the other to say "No" and go on feeling upset. Instead, trust your instincts that something *is* wrong. And state it that way. You might approach Jean and say, "Jean, you have really been quiet lately, and I realize that something is bothering you. I'd feel less tension between us if you'd share with me what it is." This way you are already telling her you are with her, understanding that something is going on for her. That understanding makes it easier for her to tell you. Also, you are not really giving her a chance to say "No, nothing's wrong" when you know something is.

So speak directly. Don't try communicating through your behaviors, your sighs, your withdrawal or your dirty looks. Enter the conflict directly and immediately. You will be surprised how small your conflicts will remain.

Principle 17

To overcome conflict as well as to prevent it in the future, create common goals you can work on together.

In more intimate relationships, a sense of partnership stands as one of your most important needs. You want the sense of walking through life with another. No matter what occurs, the two of you together can deal with what comes your way. When conflicts arise in closer relationships, your sense of partnership gets destroyed easily. You feel as though you walk alone. Getting back together on any level helps restore the feeling of partnership. And once that feeling is restored, all your other conflicts appear small and manageable.

Two groups of Boy Scouts were pitted against each other during camp. They competed in everything, from whose tents were the cleanest to who could swim the fastest. As camp wore on, bad blood developed between these two groups. Then one day the water dam broke and flooded the entire camp. All the boys had to pitch in together to save the food, clothing and equipment. They worked together on a goal bigger than either group's own goals. They needed each other. By the time the camp was restored and the equipment saved, the boys had become friends again. A goal they could agree on and cooperate over brought them back together.

The same dynamic works in any personal or work relationship. In marital relationships discussing and working together for common goals serves as a strong bond for the partnership. Here's a list of areas where common goals can be reached in a marriage:

1. Financial plan.
2. Vacations as a couple and family.
3. General leisure time.
4. Parenting issues:
   a. Discipline.
   b. Developing children's skills and values.
5. School plans for children.
6. Spiritual growth and development.
7. Extended family relationships.
8. Developing adult and couple friendships.
9. Work career goals.
10. Developing personal interests and talents.
11. Sexual relationship.
12. Physical fitness:
    a. Smoking, drinking.
    b. Diet, exercise.

In a marital relationship working together, playing together, dreaming together all create the sense of partnership that reduces hurtful conflict. In the work area creating common work goals and focusing on them tends to draw employees together. The goal must be strong enough to draw the workers to it. Having goals in common brings you together cooperatively.

Principle 18

Resolve conflict by using GRIT.

GRIT stands for the "Gradual Reduction In Tension." This notion was first presented by a social psychologist, Charles Osgood, Ph.D. in the late 1950s. He was studying international conflict and realized that nations always perceived other nations as the "aggressors" and their own nation as seeking peace. He became convinced that to resolve such conflicts, you had to change the other nation's perception of you as the aggressor. You had to demonstrate that you were a peace-loving and cooperative nation. By showing that face consistently, the other nation would gradually change its view of you as "being against" it and would then begin to trust your good will. That nation, then, would begin acting more cooperatively and peacefully toward you.

Perhaps the most dramatic example of this principle in action occurred in recent times between the Soviet Union and the United States. Beginning in the late 1980s the Soviet Union began changing its behavior toward the West. It started reducing arms unilaterally and making other concessions that could not be interpreted as "against the U.S." It began acting peacefully. In a very short time American citizens, who once feared and hated the Soviets, hailed their leader as a man of peace. As we changed our perception of the Soviets, we also began making gestures that suggested cooperation with them. As time passed a "Gradual Reduction In Tension" between these two nations occurred and continues today.

In interpersonal relationships GRIT also can be used. First of all, realize that you will employ this strategy only in those relationships that are very important to you and that you want to keep. You will not make this heroic effort in unimportant relationships. Second, you need to recognize that the other person considers you the "bad guy" or the "aggressor." Thus, your goal will be to change his or her perception of you as the enemy. You will attempt to alter that individual's view of you to one of a cooperative, peaceful person who has the good of the other person in mind.

Now here's the heroic part. In trying to demonstrate that you are on the same side as the other, you must make *unilateral* moves toward peace. In other words, you must only concentrate on giving to the other in a caring and loving way *without any consideration of return*. You cannot look for "what he will do for me." Remember, you are trying to change his view of you as the "bad guy." The strategy of doing something for him, and then waiting to see if he will do something for you will not work. You will quit doing for him before he can change his attitude toward you. Making him believe you aren't against him takes some time. You're trying to gain his trust. So don't look for any return. Just keep giving in a caring way. Gradually, he will begin to trust you and then will respond toward you in a more cooperative way as well.

If you absolutely need a time limit on this process, give yourself three months. For three months work hard at giving and responding to him without any expectation of return. Look for nothing back. Look only at how you can give. If after three months he is still not responding, then he might be using you just to satisfy his own needs. At that point you can stop and wonder if he will ever be able to respond to you in a loving and caring way. Then you may need to make other decisions regarding your relationship.

Often when conflicts occur and don't get resolved immediately, you tend to drop out all the little supports of the friendship as well. You no longer ask the other if he wants a cup of coffee while getting your own. You don't ask how her day went. You don't tell him you're going to the drug store but just leave the house. Pulling out these little friendship supports seriously hurts the relationship. With GRIT, you keep these supports in no matter what the conflict is. You keep acting in a positive, caring way. You can see why this process is called GRIT. It takes a lot of grit and courage to do it, especially when you don't feel like being nice.

Principle 19

In a conflict of needs, compromise. In a conflict of values, understand, influence and accept.

Conflicts involve needs or values, sometimes both. In a conflict of need, what you want interferes with what the other wants. You want to watch the evening news on television, she wants to watch an old-time movie. You both want something different. You run into these conflicts with some regularity, especially in a family setting. You need the car but so does your son. You need some peace and quiet, your daughter needs her music at volume ten. At work you need to end the meeting by three o'clock, your boss needs to discuss a few more items.

Conflicts of need can be resolved by *compromise*. The notion of compromise includes the idea of both parties "losing" a little bit in order to "win" more. The goal of compromise is to create a win-win situation. The question you ask is, "How can we both win?" How can we both get our needs met here? You're not trying to beat the other person but attempting to help her win while you win as well.

You both need the car. In fact, the real need is to get some place. How can you both get to where you want to go in the easiest possible way? After discussing the issue, you may compromise by suggesting your son take the car and drop you off at your destination. But since you will be finished earlier, he can come and get you and then return to his activity. You lose a little by giving up the car; your son loses a little by having to come and get you early. But you both win as well.

Another way of resolving a conflict of need is assessing who has the greater need and meeting that need. You want to watch the news, but your wife wants to watch the old-time movie. If it's one she has already begun watching or has anticipated seeing for a long time, you may decide her need to see the movie is greater than your need to see the news. In that case you can choose to respond to her need and let go of your own. In any loving relationship this dynamic occurs frequently. It becomes an act of love for the other. It works well as long as *both* parties are willing to place the other's need before their own some of the time. However, if you are always giving in to her and don't feel she ever considers your needs, then you will become resentful of resolving your conflicts this way.

Generally, though, your first effort should be to make *both* of you winners. Even in the case with the television, you might make a compromise. With a videotape machine you can easily create ways where both of you can see the shows of your choice. You just need to watch them at different times.

Conflicts of value present a different problem. You cannot compromise your values. So you can't lose a little of your values in order for both of you to win. Here you first need to understand each other. Once you have listened to and respected the other's view, you can both attempt to influence and persuade each other to come around to your side, where the view is so much better! If you can't get the other person to see and accept your point of view, then all you can do is *accept* the difference between you.

Politics, religion, sports, philosophy, ethics and morality all offer areas that create significant conflicts of value. If you cannot persuade the other through the power of reason, then you must eventually accept and respect the differences between you and learn to live with them. Many of the issues between parents and children involve value differences. They don't allow for compromise. Some of the key conflicts include: studies, drinking, sex, drugs, music, movies, friends, religion, future careers and cars. As parents you can order children not to drink or hang around with certain kids. But you can't change their values about those issues by force.

Even in value conflicts you can sometimes get compromise going. You realize the more you order your children not to associate with a certain group, the more likely they are to do so. That's a difference in what you value. You can attempt to influence your children toward other kids. But ultimately you need to accept the difference in your taste and theirs for friends. Once you accept the difference, you might then work toward a compromise whereby your son brings his friends around to your house once in a while so you can get to know them. You might even find out they aren't such bad kids after all. (I'm not promising that, but at least you're being open to find a compromise.)

In dealing with conflicts, then, first decide if this is a conflict of *need* or a conflict of *value*. If you both have needs, then your goal is to make both of you winners. If you differ over a value or a point of view, then you must try to understand and respect the other's view. After you have understood, you can attempt to persuade and influence that person. If your persuasion works, fine. If it doesn't, you need to accept that both of you have different views and then live with the differences.

Don't be so adamant in your view that you get to the point of rejecting the other person because she doesn't agree with you. No issue is big enough, especially within the family, to break up a relationship over. If you can't win a value argument, learn to let go of your need to get your way. Hold onto the undercurrent of love between you. Sometimes parents kick their children out of the house or refuse to talk with them because of major differences. Don't allow that to happen. You can hold onto your own values, but you can't insist that anyone else hold those same values.

Principle 20

Understand and work through the natural process for resolving interpersonal conflicts.

You instinctively go through certain steps in your effort to resolve the conflicts you have with others. You never learned these steps in school. They came quite naturally to you. I want you to understand what the steps are so that you can use them consciously.

When a conflict arises, you have five basic options. Normally, you will follow these steps in this order:

Steps in Resolving Conflict

1. Change the other person.
2. Change yourself in order to change the other.
3. Change yourself in order to meet your own goals.
4. Accept the other as he/she is.
5. Leave the situation.

In most conflicts you believe the problem is the other person's, or, if it is your problem, the other is causing it. So your first step is to invite the other to change. "Would you please stop popping your gum while I'm reading? Thank you." "Would you mind not smoking in my office? Thank you." You try, in a direct way, to get the other person to do something he's not doing or to stop something he is doing. If that works, your conflict is resolved.

If that doesn't work, then you go to step 2. You try changing the way *you* have been acting in order to engineer a different response from the other person. This is sometimes referred to as "manipulation." But in a system where both of you have created the conflict, change is created when one of you – either one – does something differently. A change in you begets a change in the other. Here you ask yourself, "What can I do differently that will allow Jay to act differently?" So you decide to go with him to the in-laws without complaining, hoping this will please him and move him to go with you to your high school reunion. One change causes another. If this works, then your conflict is resolved. If any changes you make don't result in the change you want, then you go to step 3.

In step 3 you identify your own needs and seek to get them met in whatever way you can. You no longer focus on changing the other. You decide you must become more independent of him in terms of getting your needs met. You take care of your needs without looking to him. This is a dramatic step to take in a relationship. It involves some grieving, because you are losing the hope that this relationship will fulfill most of your personal needs. Now you realize it won't. Instead, you must meet your needs in different ways.

To do this with some grace you need to recognize that your own needs are important, and he simply cannot meet them. You can't go about this with a "sour grapes" attitude. You can't let yourself think, "Well, forget him. I'm just going to do whatever I want and hold it against him for the rest of our lives." You need the mental discipline to simply concentrate on your needs and goals. If you have always wanted to go back to school for some particular training, then do it. If you need friendship, then work on getting it with others. If you have a career, work to improve and develop it. This step is very difficult to keep up for a long time, because you may continue wanting something from your partner. To successfully accomplish this step, you usually need to work at it along with step 4.

Step 4 involves *acceptance*. If you can't change the other person, you ultimately must accept him as he is. If you choose to stay in the relationship, then acceptance of his limitations is necessary. But you can accept his limitations only if you find other things about the relationship to be valuable. You might say, "There are so many other nice things about Jay that I can live with this one problem." Or you might say, "I cannot leave this relationship because of our children or for financial reasons, so I can accept his limitations for these other values." Acceptance is difficult on a sustained basis. Your ability to appreciate the strengths and weaknesses of your partner helps. In a marriage remember you took him "for better and for worse." There are some "for worses." You may need to accept those in order to have the "for betters."

Finally, if you can't accept the other person's behavior because it causes you pain and suffering, and you cannot change him, then your only other option is to *leave*. This should always be the last option. Make sure you have seriously worked through the first four steps and have not been successful. Only if all else has failed does leaving become the inevitable choice. If you have honestly struggled to invite him to change, attempted to change yourself, attempted to meet your own needs in other ways and diligently tried to accept him as he is, and none of that has worked, then you can, with a clear sense of integrity, choose to leave the relationship. You have gone the extra mile. You have done all you know to do. In order not to destroy yourself, then, you need to leave the relationship. Remember, though, leaving should be the last step, not the first step.

By working through this process, you hope the conflict ends before you reach the leaving stage. With the skills you have gained from reading this book and practicing these attitudes and behaviors, you should rarely need to get to step 5 – leaving. Most of your conflicts can be resolved in steps 1 and 2. If you deal with conflicts by entering them quickly and directly; if you are comfortable with yourself and don't react in a defensive way; if you avoid attacking the other person but instead look for win-win resolutions, you will almost always resolve your conflicts before they become international incidents.

Conflict comes with the territory of living in relationships. It can lead to great pain and isolation, or it can move you to ever-deeper union. It all depends on how you respond to it. My hope for you is that you enter your conflicts as an opportunity to learn about yourself and the other, and that your conflicts lead you to a greater sense of partnership. The more you actively work to resolve the conflicts that arise for you, the fewer conflicts you will find surfacing in your life.

Chapter Four

Developing this Skill
with Others

You will learn the skill of resolving conflict best by your reflection on real conflicts. You may do this somewhat instinctively already. You have a major difference with your friend. You fight. Then afterward you make up. As part of the making-up you discuss what happened to cause the fight. That time of reflection on "what happened" becomes your moment of learning. You begin to understand your own responses, the other person's reactions and the dynamics that went on between you.

Such awareness teaches you about your choices the next time a conflict arises. You will become aware that you need not try persuading him while he is trying to persuade you. Your awareness helps you realize that you can slow yourself down, listen well to him, receive his message and then – only after he has finished telling you what he needs – let him know what you need.

Awareness of what you're thinking and doing while in conflict automatically slows you down and allows you to consider several alternatives to your natural response – a response that may have fueled the conflict in the past. Awareness leads to choices, and choices lead to change. To increase your awareness of conflict, it helps to work with another person or a group of people.

Here are some steps for discussion on how to increase your conflict-resolution skills by reflecting with others.

Step One

Each of you brings to the group a recent conflict you have experienced. Take one at a time and tell your story. Try to make it short. You need not get into all the tiny details. Give enough, though, so that the significant dynamics become clear. At this point you're trying to "objectively" lay out what happened. Don't accuse anyone or try to get group members "on your side." The group isn't a judge and jury. The members want only to understand *what happened*, not whose fault it was.

After you share your story, the group can help you identify the *causes* of the conflict. Look at the expectations you had of the other that turned into demands. See if you were creating a win-lose situation, seeking power and control, responding too quickly, polarizing, dramatizing, personalizing and so on. Your job at this point is to learn what caused this conflict.

Each member of the group should present a conflict and seek to understand what caused it.

Step Two

Next role-play the conflict in a more constructive way, attempting to use "Giving-Receiving" skills of communication. Practice *slowing down* your responses so you learn to listen. As you practice listening, try to identify what the other person *needs*. Remember, unmet needs are always the basic cause of interpersonal conflict. Let the other know what you heard. Check to see if you truly understand what the other needs from you. The group can help you identify the other's needs.

Step Three

Identify and discuss your own unmet needs in this situation. Then role-play expressing your needs in an "asking" way instead of in a "demanding" way. Also practice sending "I messages" instead of "you messages."

Step Four

In future sessions assess your basic attitudes about conflict.Through discussion try to identify your beliefs when you get into conflict. Observe how defensive you become. What do you think makes you so defensive? Observe how aggressive you get. What thoughts do you have that cause your aggressive reactions? Understanding how you think during conflict helps you know what you need to change.

Step Five

Spend sessions on finding new, more helpful thoughts to replace those that keep you defensive or aggressive in conflict. Use this book to identify more helpful thoughts. Discuss them. Try to make them your own.

Step Six

Discuss different action steps you can take in conflict, such as dealing with issues immediately and directly. Decide on a particular action step that you intend to employ the next time conflict arises. Role-play and practice it in the group. This will give you confidence in employing the step in a real conflict situation.

Step Seven

You can take a conflict and apply the five steps people use to resolve conflict (see page 51). See if you have gone through those steps one by one. What step are you on now? What strategies have you used to change the other? to get your needs met? to accept what you cannot change?

Conclusion

Working with another person or a group will assist you in learning the skills for resolving conflict. If you can't find a group or another person (whether a professional or a friend), you can use the same steps on your own. Taking time to reflect on what causes you to get into conflict, how you think during conflict, how you can think in ways that are more helpful to you, and how you can choose to respond to conflict will certainly improve your ability to handle the common conflicts that surface in your life.

Your private or group reflection increases your awareness. Awareness gives you options that free you from habitually responding to conflict in the same unworkable ways. Through awareness and practice you will no longer get stuck in destructive patterns of conflict that cause so much anguish within you and lead to the breakdown of a relationship that has yielded much good.

If you know how to work with conflict, your desire and longing to be connected and intimate with other people will be fulfilled. Conflicts will inevitably enter your life. But if you learn to enter the conflict, look for what you both need and try to make both of you winners, you will find the intimacy and love you deeply crave.

Appendix

Review of Principles for Resolving Conflict

1. In the midst of conflict slow down so you can learn rather than persuade.
2. Create a *Giver-Receiver* rhythm of communication when you have differences.
3. Don't get hooked by people's first statements to you. Keep searching for the real and deeper meaning of what they say.
4. Move into rather than away from conflict.
5. Realize that objective truth will never be known.
6. Realize the other actually believes he or she is right.
7. Free yourself from *blaming* the other. Realize it takes two of you to make a conflict happen.
8. Bring a light heart and a flexible mind to all your conflicts.
9. During a conflict, know that the other person's words make a statement about him or her, not about you.
10. Realize that another's words do not make or change *your* reality.

11. Stay with the present issue; do not use the past as ammunition.
12. Never attack the other person. Keep away from his or her vulnerable spots.
13. When presenting a difficulty to your partner, own your own problem and talk about *you,* not the other.
14. In a conflict, keep your statements reality-based. Do not dramatize in order to make a point.
15. Deal with issues *immediately.*
16. Deal with issues directly, not indirectly.
17. To overcome conflict as well as to prevent it in the future, create common goals you can work on together.
18. Resolve conflict by using GRIT.
19. In a conflict of needs, compromise. In a conflict of values, understand, influence and accept.
20. Understand and work through the natural process for resolving interpersonal conflicts.